AN ILLUSTRATED DATA GUIDE TO

SUBMARINES
OF
WORLD WAR II

Compiled by
Christopher Chant

TIGER BOOKS INTERNATIONAL
LONDON

This edition published in 1997 by
Tiger Books International PLC
Twickenham

Published in Canada in 1997 by
Vanwell Publishing Limited
St. Catharines, Ontario

© Graham Beehag Books
Christchurch
Dorset

Printed in Hong Kong

ISBN 1-85501-865-9

CONTENTS

'Saphir' class
(France)

Type: Sea-going minelaying submarine

Displacement: 761 tons surfaced and 925 tons submerged

Dimensions: Length 216ft 2.5in (65.90m); beam 23ft 4.5in (7.12m); draught 14ft 1in (4.30m)

Armament: One 2.95in (75mm) gun, three 21.65in (550mm) torpedo tubes (two bow and one stern) with 5 torpedoes, two 15.75in (400mm) torpedo tubes in a trainable mounting with 2 torpedoes, and 32 mines

Propulsion: Two Normand-Vickers diesel engines delivering 1,300hp (969kW) and two electric motors delivering 1,100hp (820kW) to two shafts

Performance: Maximum speed 12kt surfaced and 9kt submerged; radius 7,000nm (8,060 miles; 12,970km) surfaced at 7.5kt and 80nm (92 miles; 148km) submerged at 4kt

Complement: 42

The French navy was similar to the Royal Navy of the early 1930s in having a six-boat class of minelaying submarines, namely the Saphir class built between 1925 and 1931 at the Toulon Naval Dockyard. These boats were much smaller than their British counterparts, however, as they were designed for Mediterranean rather than North Sea and Atlantic operations. A particular constraint on the design was the fact that the French had not designed a mine for launch through a standard torpedo tube, so the design of the hull was dominated by the mine stowage. This had been developed by Normand, one of France's best-known submarine constructors, and was based essentially on that of the British E class minelaying submarine class of 1914—18. Thus the space between the widely separated double hulls had 16 vertical chutes built into it as four groups of four, and each chute could carry two mines for a total of 32 sea-laid mines. A particular weakness of this obsolescent arrangement was that the mines had to be of a special design that could not readily be used by other launchers. The British, it should be noted, had foregone the system in favour of a stern-laying system for mines stowed in the upper casing.

One of six 'Saphir' class minelaying submarines of the French navy, the Perle is seen before the outbreak of World War II, in which the submarine performed with very great distinction and considerable operational success. The boat survived the war and was scrapped in 1949.

Four stretched boats, continuing the jewel name theme, were planned as the units of the 'Emeraude' class. These were to have followed the 'Saphir' class in the period between 1931 and 1938, and with a hull lengthened by 22ft 11.5in (7.0m) would have carried 40 rather than 32 mines. In the event, only the first boat was laid down, and it was destroyed on the slip during the German occupation of France in the early summer of 1940.

Of the six 'Saphir' class submarines, the *Nautilus* was sunk in Bizerta harbour by Allied bombing during January 1943; the *Saphir* and the *Turquoise* were seized in Bizerta harbour by Axis forces and pressed into short-term Italian service (the *Saphir* was scuttled in Naples harbour in September 1943 and the *Turquoise* was scuttled in Bizerta harbour in May 1943); the *Diamant* was scuttled in Toulon harbour in November 1942 to prevent its seizure by the Germans as they extended their occupation to the whole of France after the Anglo-American landings in French North-West Africa.

From June 1940 the *Rubis* and the *Perle* operated under the Free French flag, the *Perle* being sunk in error by Allied air attack during July 1944. The *Rubis* began to work with the British Home Fleet in April 1940, laying mines in Norwegian waters, and between that time and the end of 1944 the boat completed 22 successful minelaying operations, most of them designed to interrupt the coastal routes used by German merchant shipping. The total of 15 ships known to have been destroyed on her mines included several Scandinavian ships carrying ore cargoes to Germany, a minesweeper, and four small anti-submarine vessels. She also torpedoed and sank a Finnish vessel.

'Surcouf' class
(France)

Type: Ocean-going commerce-raiding submarine

Displacement: 3,210 tons surfaced and 4,250 tons submerged

Dimensions: Length 360ft 10.5in (110.00m); beam 29ft 6.5in (9.00m); draught 29ft 9in (9.01m)

Armament: Two 8in (203mm) guns in a twin turret, two 37mm AA guns in single mountings, eight 21.65in (550mm) torpedo tubes (four bow and four in a trainable mounting aft) with 14 torpedoes, four 15.75in (400mm) torpedo tubes in a trainable mounting aft with 8 torpedoes, and one Besson MB.411 floatplane

Propulsion: Two Sulzer diesel engines delivering 7,600hp (5,668kW) and two electric motors delivering 3,400hp (2,535kW)) to two shafts

Performance: Maximum speed 18kt surfaced and 8.5kt submerged; radius 10,000nm (11,515 miles; 18,530km) surfaced at 10kt and 60nm (69 miles; 111km) submerged at 5kt

Complement: 118

During and after World War I, most of the major naval powers experimented with the idea of the cruiser submarine for long-range sorties designed to intercept and destroy significant tonnages of an enemy's merchant marine. All these boats were considerably larger than usual, with good endurance in terms of fuel capacity, armament, and consumables for the crew, and some of the boats carried one or more small aircraft to increase their effective search radius.

The only design that managed to combine all these features with reasonable success in one hull was the *Surcouf* of the French navy. Ordered under the 1926 programme as the first in a class of three, the boat was built by the Cherbourg Naval Dockyard and was the only boat of its class to be completed; it was also the largest

The Surcouf has a good claim to having been the only successful specialised commerce-raiding submarine ever completed and placed in service, and for its time it was a large and advanced boat with particular capabilities provided by its combination of two large-calibre guns in a twin turret with a long-base rangefinder, two different calibres of torpedo, and provision for a scouting and gunnery-spotting floatplane.

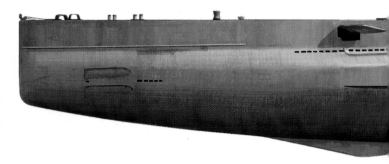

submarine in the world in terms of displacement, although it was shorter than both the American 'Narwhal' and Japanese 'A' class boats.

At the time of the Washington Naval Treaty of 1922 the British *M1*, *M2* and *M3* boats were in existence, each with a primary surface-to-surface armament of one 12in (305mm)

gun in a turret forward of the conning tower. In order to prevent further development in this direction, even though the 'M' class boats had revealed themselves to be too large for effective use and also tactically limited by their poor manoeuvrability, the treaty placed a limit of 8in (203mm) on the calibre of main gun that could be carried by any future

Designed for long-range operations against merchant vessels with only limited warship escort, the Surcouf had a maximum diving depth of only 260ft (80m). Among the boat's provisions was a boarding launch with a speed of 17kt and a range of 61nm (70 miles; 113km), and a compartment for the incarceration of up to 40 prisoners.

submarine. Only the French fitted the 8in main gun, and only in the *Surcouf*, which carried two such guns in a complicated pressure-tight twin turret located forward of the conning tower. The magazine for the main armament carried 600 shells, and these could be fired to a maximum range of 30,185yds (27,600m) at a gun elevation of 30° with the aid of a rangefinder possessing a base length of 39ft 4in (12.00m). The turret could open fire 2½ minutes after the boat had surfaced.

Faired into the after portion of the conning tower was another pressure-tight section abaft, in this instance for the accommodation of one Besson MB.411 floatplane. This diminutive scouting aeroplane was designed specifically for this application, and had to be taken out of the hangar before the wings could be attached and the whole floatplane lowered into the water for take-off: this was a time-consuming and dangerous operation that had to be reversed when the floatplane was recovered at the end of a sortie. The concept may have been acceptable in 1926 when it was first mooted, but was neither effective nor acceptable by the time of World War II.

The nature and disposition of the torpedo armament was peculiarly French. This armament was based on four 21.65in (550mm) fixed tubes in a conventional bow arrangement, with six reload weapons; four 21.65in (550mm) tubes in a trainable quadruple mounting in the casing three-quarters aft, without reload weapons; and four 15.75in (400mm) tubes in a trainable quadruple mounting in the casing right aft, with four reload weapons. The 15.75in (400mm) torpedoes were intended specifically for use against merchant shipping, and although fast they had a range of only 1,530yds (1,400m).

The boat was also fitted initially with a 16kt boarding launch (that was later removed), and had a secure compartment for 40 captured seamen.

The mode of operation for submarines such as these was never fully defined, and the *Surcouf* was never identified with a particular role. Seized by the British in Plymouth in July 1940, she was operated by a Free French crew on several Atlantic patrols. In December 1941 the boat, in company with three French corvettes, was involved in the seizure of the Vichy French islands of St Pierre and Miquelon in the St Lawrence estuary on Canada's eastern seaboard. The *Surcouf* sank in the Gulf of Mexico in February 1942, after being rammed by a merchant vessel.

'Type II' class
(Germany)

Type: Coastal patrol and minelaying submarine

Displacement: 314 tons surfaced and 364 tons submerged

Dimensions: Length 144ft 2in (43.95m); beam 16ft 0in (4.81m); draught 12ft 9in (3.90m)

Armament: One 20mm AA cannon later increased to four 20mm AA cannon in two twin mountings, and three 21in (533mm) torpedo tubes (all forward) for 6 torpedoes or 8 mines

Propulsion: Two diesel engines delivering 700hp (522kW) and two electric motors delivering 410hp (306kW) to two shafts

Performance: Maximum speed 13kt surfaced and 7.5kt submerged; radius 3,510nm (4,040 miles; 6,500km) surfaced at 12kt and 56.5nm (65 miles; 105km) submerged at 4kt

Complement: 25

In 1935 Germany repudiated the terms of the Treaty of Versailles that had ended her part in World War I and included among its provisions a ban on German construction and operation of submarines. The repudiation forced the rapid negotiation of an Anglo-German agreement which permitted Germany to build submarines with a total displacement no greater than 45 per cent of the submarine force operated by the Royal Navy. A major task now facing Karl Dönitz, the commander of the German navy's new submarine arm, was to divide this total tonnage into the precise numbers and types of boat that would provide the basis for an effective wartime submarine capability. One of the requirements that was soon identified was that for a coastal submarine roughly equivalent to the later 'UB' classes that operated successfully in British waters during World War I. During the 'submarine holiday' imposed by the Treaty of Versailles, German design expertise had been maintained through work for export, and the prototype for the 'Type IIA' class was the *Vesikko*, a boat built in Finland during 1933 to a German design based on a combination of features from the 'UB II' and later 'UF' classes of World War I.

The 'Type IIA' class had surfaced and submerged displacements of 254 and 303 tons respectively on an overall length of 134ft 3in (40.92m), and proved to be manoeuvrable with a crash-dive time of only 25 seconds. The boats' profile and lively surface characteristics earned them the nickname 'canoes'.

Although the small displacement of the 'Type IIA' class would have permitted the construction of a large number of such boats within Germany's tonnage total, the design was very limited in operational terms as a result of its surfaced and submerged radii of 910 and 30nm (1,050 and 35 miles;

The U-18 was a 'Type IIB' coastal submarine built by Germania Werft at Kiel and launched in December 1935. The boat arrived in the Black Sea during World War II but was scuttled at Constanta as the Soviet forces arrived in September 1944.

1,690 and 56km) respectively, so the basic type was steadily evolved and improved in successive 'Type IIB', 'Type IIC' and 'Type IID' variants, the specification above referring to the last variant. The 'Type IIB' class had an overall length of 140ft 0in (42.67m) for greater bunkerage and radius; the 'Type IIC' class was modelled on the 'Type IIB' but had more powerful engines, greater bunker volume and more powerful electric motors for a submerged speed of 7kt; and the 'Type IID' had saddle tanks. The design was based on a single hull with a trim tank at each end of the pressure hull as well as an internal 'rapid dive' tank amidships As only three torpedo tubes were fitted with a strictly limited number of reload torpedoes, a load of eight mines was an alternative rather than an addition.

As the emphasis of submarine warfare was moving from coastal to sea-going operations from the late 1930s, construction of the 'Type II' class submarines ended in 1941, the boats thereafter being operated mainly in the training and trials roles, including early experimentation with snorkelling equipment. Total production amounted to 6 'Type IIA', 20 'Type IIB', 8 'Type IIC' and 16 'Type IID' class boats.

'Type VII' class
(Germany)

Type: Sea-going attack submarine

Displacement: 769 tons surfaced and 871 tons submerged

Dimensions: Length 218ft 2in (66.50m); beam 20ft 4in (6.20m); draught 15ft 7in (4.15m)

Armament: One 3.465in (88mm) gun, one 37mm AA gun, two 20mm AA cannon in single mountings later increased to eight 20mm AA cannon in four twin mountings, and five 21in (533mm) torpedo tubes (four forward and one aft) for 14 torpedoes

Propulsion: Four diesel engines delivering 2,800hp (2,088kW) and two electric motors delivering 750hp (559kW) to two shafts

Performance: Maximum speed 11.5kt surfaced and 7.5kt submerged; radius 8,500nm (9,785 miles; 15,150km) surfaced at 10kt and 81nm (93 miles; 150km) submerged at 4kt

Complement: 44

In a manner closely analogous to that of the 'Type II' class, the 'Type VII' class submarine had its origins in a design prepared for the export market, namely the 'Vetehinen'

The 'Type VIIC' class boats were Germany's most important sea-going submarines in the first half of World War II, and proved highly effective in the eastern Atlantic.

class that was built by Finland in 1930–31 and was itself derived from the German 'UB III' class of 1918. To permit the greatest possible number of hulls to be built within the tonnage limitation imposed by the Anglo-German naval agreement, the 10 examples of the 'Type VIIA' class were limited to a length of 220ft 3in (67.13m) and surfaced/-submerged displacements of 626/745 tons. It was important to optimise performance and offensive capability; internal volume was maximised by mounting the after tube in the casing (where it could be reloaded only with difficulty and only when the boat was surfaced), and by accommodating spare torpedoes and part of the bunker capacity externally, where they were vulnerable to the effect of depth-charge attack.

It was then appreciated that the 'Type VIIA' class placed too much capability into insufficient length and displacement, so the following 'Type VIIB' and 'Type VIIC' class boats were stretched to a length of 218ft 3in (66.53m) and 220ft 3in (67.13m) respectively for surfaced/submerged displacements of 753/857 tons and 769/871 tons, as a means of increasing internal volume and to allow the installation of more-powerful diesel engines for higher surfaced speed. These modified boats were highly successful, nearly 700 units being built in various subvariants until the end of World War II. The specification above applies to the 'Type VIIC' class.

Later improvements included greater diving depth, a reinforced conning tower, improved AA armament in an effort to defeat the attentions of radar-equipped Allied warplanes that sought to interdict the German submarine arm's surfaced transit routes between the bases and their operational areas, and snorkels: all of these features reflected the Allies' development and implementation of improved anti-submarine systems and tactics. Significantly, moreover, most of the boats were completed without a deck gun as surface operations became impossible

All the boats had provision for the laying of mines through their standard 21in (533mm) torpedo tube. These weapons could not guarantee a sinking rather than a disablement of the target, however, and in an effort to create a capability for the laying of the largest type of moored mine, six 'Type VII' boats were stretched to the 'Type VIID' standard by the addition of a 32ft 9.75in (10.0m) section amidships containing five vertical free-flooding tubes, each accommodating three complete mine assemblies. These tubes extended upward to the 01 deck level in an extended conning tower. Another four boats of the 'Type VIIF' subclass were similarly lengthened, but the extra volume was allocated to spare torpedoes that could be transferred at sea as a means of extending the operational duration of other boats. Up to 25 torpedoes could be carried, but the transfer process (with both boats motionless on the surface) became increasingly dangerous, and was therefore abandoned. The 'Type VIIE', a study in improved propulsion, progressed no further than the drawing board.

The 'Type VIIC' class was perfectly conventional by the standards of its day but was comparatively small for the sea-going role, and therefore possessed a low level of habitability as a result of bunker and food storage requirements, and needed to embark a large number of reload torpedoes.

'Type IX' class
(Germany)

Type: Ocean-going attack submarine

Displacement: 1,120 tons surfaced and 1,232 tons submerged

Dimensions: Length 251ft 8in (76.70m); beam 22ft 2in (6.75m); draught 15ft 5in (4.70m)

Armament: One 4.13in (105mm) gun, one 37mm AA gun, one 20mm AA cannon, and six 21in (533mm) torpedo tubes (four forward and two aft) for 22 torpedoes

Propulsion: Four diesel engines delivering 4,400hp (3,281kW) and two electric motors delivering 1,000hp (746kW) to two shafts

Performance: Maximum speed 18.2kt surfaced and 7.5kt submerged; radius 13,490nm (15,535 miles; 25,000km) surfaced at 10kt and 62nm (71.5 miles; 115km) submerged at 4kt

Complement: 48

The 'Type IX' class of German submarines was designed specifically for the oceanic warfare role. Generally based on the smaller 'Type II' class design, it differed fundamentally in having a double hull. This feature increased useful internal volume by enabling fuel and ballast tanks to be sited externally, and in turn the extra hull improved survivability by cushioning the inner (pressure) hull from explosive shock and also gave the boats greatly improved surfaced characteristics. Habitability for long-endurance operations was considerably improved over that of earlier classes, and 22 torpedoes were shipped – about 50 per cent more than were carried by the 'Type VIIC' class. The deck gun was increased in calibre from 3.465in (88mm) to 4.13in (105mm) for improved lethality and greater stand-off range.

In common with other classes, the 'Type IX' class was considerably developed in the course of a large-scale production effort throughout World War II: whereas the 'Type IXA' and 'Type VIIA' classes were 251ft 0in (76.50m) and 211ft 7.5in (64.50m) in length respectively, the ultimate 'Type IXD' and 'Type VIIF' classes were 287ft 1in (87.50m) and 254ft 7in (77.6m) in length.

The 'Type IXC' class ocean-going submarine was a development of the 'Type IXB' class, with greater operational radius provided by the increased use of the external tanks for greater bunkerage. The habitability of these boats was better than that of the 'Type VII' class sea-going submarines.

The major factor driving the evolution of the 'Type IX' class was the desire to improve range rather than offensive capability. Whilst the eight 'Type IXA' class boats could achieve a radius of 10,525nm (12,115 miles; 19,500km) on the surface at 10kt, even before the outbreak of World War II the boats were being complemented by the first of 14 'Type IXB' class boats capable of 12,005nm (13,825 miles; 22,250km). These were followed by the largest group, the 'Type IXC' and the slightly modified 'Type IXC40' classes totalling 149 boats with bunkers for a radius of 13,490nm (15,535 miles; 25,000km).

From the beginning of World War II the 'Type IX' class boats worked the western and southern parts of the Atlantic Ocean and, after America's entry into the war in December 1941, were supplemented by 'Type VIIC' class submarines for the so-called 'happy time', in which they decimated the shipping that plied the USA's eastern seaboard to and from the Caribbean before a proper convoy system had been established.

As early as 1940, the 'Type IXD' class was being planned with a 35ft 5in (10.80m) integrated section. Two examples of the 'Type IXD1' class were built without armament, but were capable of stowing over 250 tons of fuel for the topping-up of other boats. The 29 submarines of the following 'Type IXD2' class were operational boats with an impressive range of 31,515nm (36,290 miles; 58,400km) that allowed them to operate in the Indian Ocean and even as far as Japan. Some included a small single-seat towed gyro-kite to increase their visual search radius. The 'Type IXD2' class was further refined in the 'Type IXD2-42' class, but only one of this variant was completed. The use of advanced diesel engines in the 'Type IXD1' class submarines provided a 21kt surface speed, but the engines were found to be unreliable and were not used in other boats.

'Type X' and 'Type XI' classes
(Germany)

Type: Ocean-going minelaying submarine

Displacement: 1,163 tons surfaced and 2,177 tons submerged

Dimensions: Length 294ft 7in (89.80m); beam 30ft 2in (9.20m); draught 13ft 6in (4.11m)

Armament: One 4.13in (105mm) gun that was later removed, one 37mm AA gun, one 20mm AA cannon later increased to four 20mm AA cannon in two twin mountings, two 21in (533mm) torpedo tubes (both aft) for 15 torpedoes, and 66 mines

Propulsion: Four diesel engines delivering 4,200hp (3,132kW) and two electric motors delivering 1,100hp (820kW) to two shafts

Performance: Maximum speed 16.5kt surfaced and 7kt submerged; radius 18,565nm (21,375 miles; 34,400km) surfaced at 10kt and 95nm (109 miles; 175km) submerged at 4kt

Complement: 52

Of the five principal types of submarine identified by the German naval staff in its requirements before the start of World War II, the attack submarines with short-, medium- and long-endurance capabilities became the 'Type II', 'Type VII' and 'Type IX' classes respectively, while the 'small' minelayer and long-range cruiser submarines were then modified in concept to become the 'Type X' and 'Type XI' classes respectively.

Only three boats of the 'Type XI' class were built, and were very large submarines with a length of 377ft 3.5in (115.0m) and a surfaced displacement of 3,140 tons. In effect, the boats were submersible surface raiders with a high surfaced speed of 23kt; they incorporated a superstructure that provided stowage for a small reconnaissance floatplane, and carried a deck armament of

four 5in (127mm) guns, in two twin turrets located forward and abaft the conning tower, to supplement the inbuilt eight 21in (533mm) torpedo tubes (six bow and two stern) for 12 torpedoes.

The large cruiser submarine had been moderately successful in World War I, but in World War II it was rapidly revealed to be obsolete in concept, and was soon discontinued. The most notable achievement of the Type XI class boats was *U-601*s initial sighting of the British convoy JW-55B in the Norwegian Sea on Christmas Day 1943, the resulting contact report leading to the dispatch of the battle-cruiser *Scharnhorst* that was in turn intercepted by superior Royal Navy surface forces and sunk on the following day.

As it was nally schemed, the Type XA class was in fact a very large minelayer whose design incorporated multiple vertical mine stowage shafts, of the type used successfully in the Type VIID class. Considered vulnerable, probably because of its signi cant size, the Type XA class progressed no further than the drawing board and was superseded by the Type XB class, to which the above speci cation applies. These eight boats were smaller than the projected Type XA class submarines, with a circular-section pressure hull anked by a large and slab-sided outer hull. On the centreline forward, six mine storage tubes extended from keel to the top of a hump in the casing, and each of these tubes carried three moored mine assemblies. On each side, in the space between the hulls, were tted 12 shorter stowage tubes each containing two mines. The total load was 66 large mines. Built to avoid action, the Type XB class

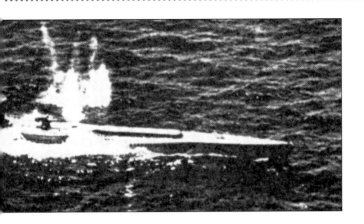

Fitted with the wholly inadequate AA armament of one 20mm cannon, the U-118 of the 'Type XB' class comes under attack from the aircraft of the American escort carrier Bogue, which depth-charged and sank this German submarine to the west of the Canary Islands in June 1943. The casing on the foredeck covered the tops of the free-flooding vertical mineshafts.

submarines had only two torpedo tubes, accommodated right aft. As events later proved, the boats were better suited to the supply role rather than the minelaying role.

The survival of Germany's submarines between operational missions was largely dependent on the use of massive reinforced concrete pens such as these at Trondheim in Norway. These were among the few that survived relatively unscathed to the end of World War II despite the Allies' bombing campaign, in which such pens were very high-priority targets.

'Type XVII' class
(Germany)

Type: Coastal attack submarine

Displacement: 312 tons surfaced and 357 tons submerged

Dimensions: Length 136ft 2in (41.50m); beam 11ft 2in (3.40m); draught 14ft 0in (4.25m)

Armament: Two 21in (533mm) torpedo tubes (both forward) for 4 torpedoes

Propulsion: One diesel engine delivering 210hp (157kW) and one Walter closed-cycle engine delivering 2,500hp (1,864kW) or one electric motor delivering 77hp (57kW) to one shaft

Performance: Maximum speed 9kt surfaced and 21.5kt submerged on Walter engine or 5kt submerged on electric motor; radius 2,995nm (3,450 miles; 5,550km) surfaced at 9kt and 113nm (130.5 miles; 210km) submerged on Walter engine or 40.5nm (46.5 miles; 70km) submerged on electric motor

Complement: 19

The 'Type XVII' class submarine paved the way for the true submarine rather than just the submersible, for although it was not totally independent of the surface in terms of its air requirements, it was nonetheless capable of a very high underwater speed with a greater range than possible in conventional battery-powered submarines.

In the middle of World War II, the Allies' introduction of anti-submarine aircraft and radar made it impossible for German submarines to use their high surface speed as a basis for attack. Continued survivability and operational utility now demanded that submarines had to be optimised for submerged performance, and only a cleaner hull design combined with machinery systems that were independent of surface air would provide adequate performance in this difficult role. The 'Type XVII' class marked this fundamental but transitional step forward in submarine capabilities.

The key to the high underwater performance of the 'Type XVII' class was the adoption of the Walter closed-cycle propulsion system: this relied on the near-explosive decomposition of concentrated hydrogen peroxide in the presence of a catalyst to create a reaction whose result was a high-temperature mix of steam and free oxygen, and into which fuel oil could be injected for a combustion process that created the high-pressure gases to drive a conventional turbine. The two major flaws in the system were the fact that any impurity could act as a catalyst to initiate the decomposition process at a disastrously early stage, and that the complete system was extremely 'thirsty'.

Two prototype boats proved the basic feasibility of the system and its associated machinery, and the system was therefore pressed into service in the 'Type XVII' class. The extreme thirst of the system demanded a very small boat with a single propeller. In the cruise regime this propeller was driven by a conventional diesel/electric combination,

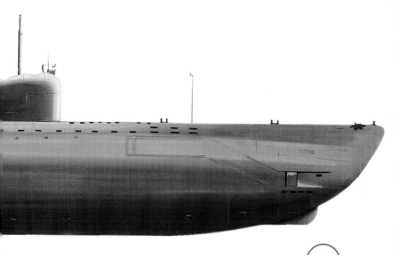

A nearly complete 'Type XVII' class Walter-powered submarine, notable externally for its cruciform control surfaces and hydrodynamically clean hull, is transferred by heavy-duty floating crane through the bomb-damaged Howaldtswerke facility at Kiel in preparation for its launch.

the Walter system being coupled-up only when it was required to force or break off from an action.

Externally the hull was cleaner than that of preceding classes, with no guns and with a minimum of protuberances. The hull was of figure-eight section with two overlapping circular pressure sections of unequal diameter. The length/beam ratio was revealed to be too high, resulting in unnecessarily high drag levels, and this meant that the 'Type XVIIA' never attained its estimated maximum speed of 25kt with two turbines on a common shaft. As a result, only four such boats were built. The modified 'Type XVIIB' class, of which three were completed to the standard detailed above, had only one turbine. Volume was available for two torpedo tubes, with just one reload for each tube, but this deficiency in torpedo numbers was offset by the increased lethality of the torpedoes.

A 'Type XVIIK' class design was projected with the volatile Walter system abandoned for conventional diesel engines aspirated with pure oxygen stored on board.

'Type XXI' class
(Germany)

Type: Ocean-going attack submarine

Displacement: 1,621 tons surfaced and 1,819 tons submerged

Dimensions: Length 251ft 8in (76.70m); beam 21ft 9in (6.62m); draught 20ft 4in (6.20m)

Armament: Four 30mm or 20mm AA cannon in two twin mountings, and six 21in (533mm) torpedo tubes (all forward) for 23 torpedoes

Propulsion: Four diesel engines delivering 4,000hp (2,983kW) and two electric motors delivering 5,000hp (3,729kW) or two electric motors delivering 226hp (169kW) to two shafts

Performance: Maximum speed 15.5kt surfaced and 16kt submerged on main electric motors or 3.5kt submerged on creeping electric motors; radius 15,540nm (17,895 miles; 28,800km) surfaced and 283nm (326 miles; 525km) submerged at 6kt

Complement: 51

Without doubt one of the most important and influential submarine designs in history, the 'Type XXI' class set performance standards that remained unsurpassed until the advent of nuclear-powered submarines a decade later. Although closed-cycle turbine and diesel powerplants had already been introduced by the Germans, both types still needed further development for operational reliability, so a temporary high-power electric boat was produced on the basis of established submarine technology. With the lower pressure hull packed with high-capacity battery cells, the 'Type XXI' class boats could develop more power submerged than surfaced, and the main propulsion motors were supplemented by low-power units for silent manoeuvring.

Like that of the 'Type XVII' class, the pressure hull of the

The clean lines and lack of external projections were the clues to the ability of the 'Type XXI' class submarine to reach and maintain a high underwater speed.

'Type XXI' class was of the 'double-bubble' figure-eight cross-section, and although this was externally framed it was prefabricated in eight sections at a variety of sites before final assembly at the shipyard. The external framing increased volume and facilitated the addition of a hydrodynamically 'clean' outer skin. Construction was of the all-welded type for a production target of three boats per week in an ambitious programme designed to yield an eventual 1,500 units (*U-2500* to *U-4000*), and to facilitate this programme almost all other submarine production was cut back or cancelled.

The boats of the 'Type XXI' class were designed to spend their full patrol time submerged, and a snorkel was fitted so that the diesel engines could be run for battery-recharge purposes. Habitability was greatly improved over that of earlier classes, and included both air-conditioning and air regeneration systems. The only guns were paired automatic weapons set into the forward and after profiles of the long 'sail' type of conning tower, and a combination of active and passive sonars was installed to allow the generation of a full solution to the torpedo fire-control problem without use of the periscope, whose above-water section could be acquired by the radar of Allied warships.

Two variants that were proposed but not built were the 'Type XXIB' and 'Type XXIC' classes, which would have increased the number of torpedo tubes from six to 12 and 18 respectively by the insertion of extra hull sections. Fortunately for the Allies, the 'Type XXI' class did not become fully operational, although several of the boats were sunk, all of them by aircraft and in home waters.

'Type XXIII' class
(Germany)

Type: Coastal attack submarine

Displacement: 232 tons surfaced and 256 tons submerged

Dimensions: Length 112ft 0in (34.10m); beam 9ft 10in (3.00m); draught 12ft 3in (3.15m)

Armament: Two 21in (533mm) torpedo tubes (both forward) for 2 torpedoes

Propulsion: One diesel engine delivering 580hp (433kW) and one electric motor delivering 600hp (447kW) or one electric motor delivering 35hp (26kW) to one shaft

Performance: Maximum speed 10kt surfaced and 12.5kt on main electric motor or 2kt submerged on creeping electric motor; radius 1,350nm (1,555 miles; 2,500km) surfaced and 175nm (202 miles; 325km) submerged at 4kt

Complement: 14

The design of the 'Type XXIII' class submarine may have been a result of German naval thinking during the later stages of World War II: that rather than searching the Atlantic Ocean for convoys, it might be operationally advantageous to lie in wait for these convoys as they moved to and from known points of arrival and departure, even though these areas would inevitably be patrolled by potent concentrations of escort warships. The 'Type XXIII' class submarine was ideal for a task of this nature as it was small and agile, admirably suited to shallow-water operations, and packed with high-capacity battery cells for maximum underwater speed.

The hull of the 'Type XXIII' class boat had a 'double-bubble' cross-section over its forward part, but this was framed internally rather than externally and was prefabricated in four sections. The lower hull was only of partial length, and contained batteries and some ballast and fuel capacity. Outer casing was abandoned except in the

The 'Type XXIII' class submarine was the coastal counterpart of the 'Type XXI' ocean-going submarine, with clean lines and high-capacity batteries for high submerged speed.

transitional zones, and this factor, together with a low reserve buoyancy (there was only a 24-ton difference between the surfaced and submerged displacements), enabled a very rapid and tactically important crash-dive, with a time of less than 10 seconds often recorded.

Even smaller than the 'Type XVII' class boats with their Walter propulsion system, the 'Type XXIII' class submarines also had a single shaft but a propeller proportionately larger in diameter for greater propulsive efficiency. Although the submarine was designed to operate in the submerged mode with air for the diesel engine supplied via a snorkel, its silhouette on the surface was very small as it comprised just a slim conning tower with the attached low casing that enclosed the snorkel induction and engine exhaust features. No guns were shipped, and the armament was limited to two torpedo tubes without reload weapons. As there was no space inboard for the standard method of loading the tubes through doors in their rear ends, the boats had to be trimmed by the stern to expose the bow caps, through which the torpedoes were then loaded. The provision of only two torpedoes was a major tactical disadvantage: all attacks had to be effected from short range, followed by a disengagement that was either very rapid or very quiet.

By the end of World War II the Germans had placed 62 examples of the 'Type XXIII' class in service, and the only losses had been caused by Allied warplanes. It was fortunate for the Allies, therefore, that no more of these boats entered service, and that the training and dedication of the submarine arm no longer equalled the advanced technology of its boats.

'Sirena', 'Perla', 'Adua' and 'Acciaio' classes
(Italy)

Type: Sea-going attack submarine

Displacement: 679–701 tons surfaced and 842–860 tons submerged

Dimensions: Length 191ft 6in (60.18m); beam 21ft 2in (6.45m); draught 15ft 5in (4.70m)

Armament: One 3.94in (100mm) gun, two 0.52in (13.2mm) machine-guns later increased to four 0.52in (13.2mm) machine-guns, and six 21in (533mm) torpedo tubes (four forward and two aft) for 12 torpedoes

Propulsion: Two diesel engines delivering 1,200hp (895kW) and two electric motors delivering 800hp (596kW) to two shafts

Performance: Maximum speed 14kt surfaced and 8kt submerged; radius 4,855nm (5,590 miles; 9,000km) surfaced at 8kt and 73nm (84 miles; 135km) submerged at 4kt

Complement: 45

Dating from a time of considerable expansion in the Italian navy's submarine arm, the 12 boats of the 'Sirena' class were also known as the '600' class for their standard displacement on the surface, and even though this figure was handsomely exceeded in the final version of the design, the boats were admirably suited to operations in the Mediterranean. The design of the 'Sirena' class had been based on that of the preceding 'Argonauta' class, but because the units of the later class were laid down before the first units of the earlier class entered service, the design of the 'Sirena' class was completed without the benefits of experience with the 'Argonauta' class. Even so, the submarines of the 'Sirena' class were simple and sturdy, and were therefore used extensively. Only one boat survived

The Bronzo was a member of the 'Acciaio' class of submarines that was related to the earlier 'Sirena', 'Perla', and 'Adua' classes, but could not be considered a remarkable type.

after the Italian armistice with the Allied powers in September 1943.

The 'Perla' class of 10 boats was essentially a repeat of the 'Sirena' class, and of these boats the *Iride* and the *Onice* served under Nationalist colours in the Spanish Civil War (1936–39). During World War II the *Iride* and the *Ambra* (victor over the British cruiser *Bonaventure*) were adapted for the carriage and deployment of the type of human torpedo known to the British as the 'chariot': in December 1942 human torpedoes launched by the *Ambra* attacked shipping in Algiers harbour, severely damaging four merchantmen in a courageous attack that was pressed home with considerable courage and determination.

The 'Adua' class of 17 boats was a virtual repeat of the 'Perla' class, and built between 1936 and 1938. Two of the boats were adapted for the human torpedo role, and the *Scirè* was used for four human torpedo attacks on Gibraltar, including a raid in September 1941 that sank two ships. In December 1941, however, the submarine launched three human torpedoes whose attacks sank the battleships *Queen Elizabeth* and *Valiant* as well as a tanker in Alexandria harbour. The submarine was finally lost in August 1942 to an armed trawler off Haifa.

The final expression of the '600' type was the slightly larger 13-boat 'Acciaio' class built in the period 194–-42.

'Cagni' class
(Italy)

Type: Ocean-going attack submarine

Displacement: 1,680 tons surfaced and 2,110 tons submerged

Dimensions: Length 288ft 5in (87.90m); beam 25ft 6in (7.76m); draught 18ft 9in (5.12m)

Armament: Two 3.94in (100mm) guns in single mountings, four 0.52in (13.2mm) machine-guns in two twin mountings, and fourteen 17.72in (450mm) torpedo tubes (eight forward and six aft) for 36 torpedoes

Propulsion: Four diesel engines delivering 4,370hp (3,259kW) and two electric motors delivering 1,800hp (1,342kW) to two shafts

Performance: Maximum speed 17kt surfaced and 8.5kt submerged; radius 10,975nm (12,430 miles; 20,000km) surfaced at 12kt and 108nm (124 miles; 200km) submerged at 3.5kt

Complement: 82

Whilst it was of moderately large size, Italy's merchant marine could not be protected on a worldwide basis by Italy's surface fleet, which was geared to high-speed operations of limited endurance, so standard trade-defence measures were impossible. Despite this fact, the four submarines of the 'Cagni' class were laid down in September and October 1939 on the outbreak of hostilities between Germany and the Anglo-French alliance. These submarines were intended specifically for the long-range commerce-raiding role, indicating that Italy presaged a commitment against the major maritime powers, even though she was not involved in the war at this time.

The 'Cagni' class boats were the largest attack submarines built for the Italian navy and, in accord with their commerce-raiding role, were armed with small 17.72in (450mm) torpedoes rather than the 21in (533mm) weapons generally preferred in naval operations. Although these small-calibre torpedoes were longer than the standard 17.72in (450mm) weapons (enabling them to carry a 441lb/200kg warhead rather than the more common 243lb/110kg warhead), this payload was considerably less than the 595lb (270kg) warhead of the larger 21in (533mm) torpedo. As the torpedoes were for use mainly against 'soft' targets such as merchant ships, however, this warhead was considered acceptable, especially as the reduced bulk of the weapon allowed each submarine to ship 36 torpedoes. An unusual feature was the fact that torpedoes could be transferred from one end of the boat to the other. Two large deck guns were also carried in order to conserve torpedoes.

Unfortunately for Italian plans, the Mediterranean sea war required the Italian navy to keep open the vital supply route between Italy and North Africa. Following heavy losses of its surface forces, the Italian navy was compelled to press its large submarines into service in this important yet taxing role. In completing 15 trips, three of the class's four boats were sunk in only three months. Only the name boat, *Ammiraglio Cagni*, was employed in its designed role but without any real success, sinking less than 10,000 gross registered tons in two long patrols.

The Ammiraglio Millo *was a member of the undistinguished 'Cagni' class, and was sunk off the coast of Sicily in March 1942 by the British submarine* Ultimatum, *one of the 'U' class boats that proved so successful in the Mediterranean.*

'Archimede' class
(Italy)

Type: Sea-going submarine

Displacement: 985 tons surfaced and 1,259 tons submerged

Dimensions: Length 231ft 4in (70.50m); beam 22ft 5in (6.83m); draught 13ft 6in (4.10m)

Armament: Two 3.94in (100m) guns in single mountings, two 0.52in (13.2mm) machine-guns, and eight 21in (533mm) torpedo tubes (four forward and four aft) for 16 torpedoes

Propulsion: Four diesel engines delivering 3,000hp (2,237kW) and two electric motors delivering 1,300hp (969kW) to two shafts

Performance: Maximum speed 17kt surfaced and 8kt submerged; radius 10,255nm (11,805 miles; 19,000km) surfaced at 8kt and 105nm (121 miles; 195km) submerged at 3kt

Complement: 55

The four submarines of the 'Archimede' class were built to a design that was basically a scaled-up version of the preceding 'Settembrini' class, with the ballast rearranged to allow an enlargement of the bunkers and also to permit the installation of a second 3.94in (100mm) deck gun for the type's sea-going role. All the submarines were launched in 1934 and, as part of their covert support of the Nationalist cause during the Spanish Civil War, the Italians transferred two boats to Spanish colours: these were the *Archimede* and the *Torricelli*, and in order to conceal the transfer, two of the following 'Brin' class submarines assumed the transferred boats' names. The 'Settembrini', 'Archimede' and 'Brin' classes formed a closely related group that was used extensively in colonial work.

Italy's entry into World War II during June 1940 resulted in the isolation of the Italian forces in East Africa, which the

British viewed as a potential threat to their communications eastward from Egypt and the Suez Canal to the Middle East and Far East, India and Australasia. The *Galilei* sank a Norwegian tanker less than a week after the outbreak of hostilities, and only two days later further confirmed its position by stopping a neutral ship for examination. On the following day the submarine was intercepted by a British anti-submarine trawler, which inflicted damage that caused the boat to fill with noxious fumes. Unable to dive, the *Galilei* fought it out on the surface. Far larger, faster and more heavily armed than its opponent, the submarine should have

The 'Archimede' class was an improved version of the 'Settembrini' class intended for the ocean-going role, with two deck guns and larger bunkers for an extended range in a role that was not really required by the Italian navy.

been successful, but the trawler's guns killed or wounded every Italian who tried to man either of the deck guns. With most of their officers dead, the demoralised crew surrendered and the boat was then repaired and assumed the British pennant P711 until its eventual disposal in 1946.

The *Torricelli*, the *Galilei*'s replacement, was also caught by British naval forces. Forced to the surface near Perim Island, the submarine engaged in a gun action with a sloop and three 'K' class destroyers, and was inevitably sunk, although not before its guns had hit both the sloop and the destroyer *Khartoum*. The hit on the destroyer apparently caused a compressed-air explosion in one of the banks of torpedo tubes, and this was followed by the detonation of a torpedo warhead, resulting in the destruction of the ship.

'RO-100' and 'RO-35' classes
(Japan)

Type: Coastal attack submarine

Displacement: 601 tons surfaced and 782 tons submerged

Dimensions: Length 199ft 10in (60.90m); beam 20ft 0in (6.10m); draught 11ft 6in (3.50m)

Armament: One 3in (76mm) gun that was often removed, and four 21in (533mm) torpedo tubes (all forward) for 8 torpedoes

Propulsion: Two diesel engines delivering 1,100hp (820kW) and two electric motors delivering 760hp (567kW) to two shafts

Performance: Maximum speed 14kt surfaced and 8kt submerged, radius 3,510nm (4,040 miles; 6,500km) surfaced at 12kt and 59.5nm (68.5 miles; 110km) submerged at 3kt

Complement: 38

In the system of nomenclature used by the Imperial Japanese navy, small- to medium-sized submarines were designated 'RO', corresponding to the letter 'B' in the Western alphabet. In the case of the 'RO-100' class, to which the above specification applies, the terms 'Kaisho' or 'Type KS' (denoting 'small') were also used.

As designed, the 'RO' classes were to have been used for limited-endurance operations in the waters around the

Used mainly for oceanic tasks in defence of Japan's island garrisons, a task for which they were ill-suited by their limited diving depth, the boats of the 'RO-35' class were cramped but nonetheless performed moderately well although all the boats were lost.

Japanese home islands, and for this reason the maximum operational diving depth was limited to 245ft (75m). The task of the boats was later extended, however, to cover the protection of the numerous islands that were acquired in the Pacific to constitute the outer perimeter of Japan's new empire. As these islands were often surrounded by deep water, the 'RO-100' boats started at a distinct disadvantage, and even their small sonar profile could not offset the submarines' poor performance: as a result, all 18 of the boats were sunk, only two of them by aircraft. The fact that one of the boats was sunk off eastern India is indicative of the endurance of its crew, for whom a maximum endurance of 21 days had been planned. No less than five of the class were destroyed on separate occasions by the American destroyer escort *England*.

The design of the 'RO-100' class was based on the earlier 'RO-33' or 'Type K5' class, but was ultimately very different from this class, and in overall size and potential was equivalent to the British 'U' class type. The boats were unsuitable for attacks on the warships that were designated as their primary targets: the boats could have operated with success against mercantile targets, but the Japanese submarine command – revealing a characteristic lack of imagination and flexibility – refused even to consider such a role.

The class of 18 'RO-100' class submarines was ordered before Japan's entry into World War II in December 1941, but despite their small size and limited construction requirements the boats were still being completed in 1944, when their obsolescence was clearly evident. Nine further units were eventually cancelled.

The parallel 'RO-35' ('Kaichu' or 'Type K6') class was built to a design that was larger than that of the 'RO-100' class, and constituted the last medium-size boats built by the Imperial Japanese navy. The boats were completed with a length of 264ft 1in (80.50m), surfaced/submerged displacements of 1,115/1,447 tons, and armament of one 3in (76mm) gun, two 25mm AA cannon and four 21in (533mm) torpedo tubes for 10 torpedoes. Of the 18 boats completed, only one survived the war. Between them, the 'RO-35' and 'RO-100' class submarines were credited with the sinking of four minor warships and six merchantmen, which represents an appalling rate of exchange for the loss of 35 boats. Some 60 additional units of the 'RO-35' class were cancelled.

'I-15' class
(Japan)

Type: Ocean-going submarine

Displacement: 2,590 tons surfaced and 3,655 tons submerged

Dimensions: Length 356ft 4in (108.60m); beam 30ft 6in (9.30m); draught 16ft 9in (5.10m)

Armament: One 5.5in (140mm) gun, two 25mm AA guns in a twin mounting, one Yokosuka E14Y1 floatplane, and six 21in (533mm) torpedo tubes (all forward) for 17 torpedoes

Propulsion: Eight diesel engines delivering 12,400hp (9,245kW) and two electric motors delivering 2,000hp (1,491kW) to two shafts

Performance: Maximum speed 23.5kt surfaced and 8kt submerged; radius 14,030nm (16,155 miles; 26,000km) surfaced at 16kt and 100nm (115 miles; 185km) submerged at 3kt

Complement: 100

Built by Kure Navy Yard and completed in November 1941, the I-26 of the 'I-15' class was sunk to the east of the Philippine Islands in October 1944, in the build-up to the climactic four-phase Battle of Leyte Gulf.

The prefix 'I', equivalent to 'A' in the Western alphabet, was used by the Imperial Japanese navy for the larger type of submarine intended for the fleet or cruising roles. These two roles were in the process of merging into a single ocean-going role, for the 'fleet' concept was an earlier British idea of using large boats with a good surface performance to act closely as an element of the surface fleet, a concept that was not successful even in World War I.

The 'I-15' class was therefore derived from two sources. The first of these was the 'Type KD' fleet submarine of the mid-1930s, capable of a 23kt surfaced speed and possessing a range suitable for a return trip across the Pacific. The other was the 'Junsen' cruiser submarine of a slightly later date, which incorporated one or two floatplanes in a pressure-tight hangar forming part of the superstructure. These aircraft were provided purely as a means of increasing the boat's scouting capability.

The class comprised 20 submarines with a 5.5in (140mm) deck gun on a large 'bandstand', and a hangar incorporated in a low streamlined structure extending (usually to the front) from the conning tower. The freeboard was high in order to improve aircraft handling in a seaway, and was made higher along the forward end of the boat by a sloping catapult track; a folding crane was also incorporated for recovery purposes. In practice the aeroplane and its equipment proved more trouble than they were worth, and several boats had all aircraft capability removed in favour of a second gun. As such, the boats were among the more successful of Japanese submarine classes, being credited with the sinking of eight warships (including the aircraft carrier *Wasp* that was torpedoed by the *I-19*) and 59 merchantmen of about 400,000 gross registered tons.

Despite these successes, the losses of 'I-15' class boats were catastrophically high, predominantly as a result of their poor submerged performance and also because they carried only three full salvoes of torpedoes. Only one of the 20 boats survived to surrender at the end of the war. A couple of the class, along with others from the similar 'I-40' ('Type B2') and 'I-54' ('Type B3') class variants totalling six and three boats respectively, were modified to carry *Kaiten* (suicide midget submarines).

'I-361', 'I-313' and 'I-351' classes
(Japan)

Type: Supply submarine

Displacement: 1,440 tons surfaced and 2,215 tons submerged

Dimensions: Length 240ft 10in (73.40m); beam 29ft 2in (8.90m); draught 15ft 5in (4.70m)

Armament: One 5.5in (140mm) gun and two 25mm AA guns

Propulsion: Two diesel engines delivering 1,850hp (1,380kW) and two electric motors delivering 1,200hp (895kW) to two shafts

Performance: Maximum speed 13kt surfaced and 6.5kt submerged; radius 11,820nm (13,610 miles; 21,900km) surfaced at 10kt and 119nm (147 miles; 220km) submerged at 3kt

Complement: 70

The well-recorded exploits of the cruisers and destroyers of the 'Tokyo Express' that were used to supply the Japanese garrison of Guadalcanal in the Solomons group in 1942–43 have overshadowed the fact that the Japanese had many other island garrisons needing support and resupply. Once the great American counter-offensive through the Pacific Ocean began to advance during 1943, many such island garrisons were bypassed as having low strategic significance. The Japanese could not contemplate the surrender of these garrisons, and with enemy forces firmly across their lines of supply, the Japanese surface forces would have enjoyed little chance of survival in any attempt to run supplies into these garrisons. As a result, the 1942 supplementary building programme included orders for 12 specialised cargo-carrying submarines known as the 'Type D1' or 'I-361' class (to which the above specification applies), after the first such unit.

Although they were not large, the boats were ungainly as their high casing provided stowage for two 42ft 8in (13.00m) landing craft abaft the conning tower. These craft were built to withstand the pressure of a dive to 200ft (60m), and could be floated on and off by trimming the submarine. Twenty tons of stores could be carried externally, with a further 60 tons as well as two large rubber boats internally. As an alternative load, 110 equipped men could be carried on short-haul trips.

By Japanese standards the submerged endurance of the boats was good, but their 60-day surfaced endurance was excessive as resupply of garrisons out to the radius of which the boats were capable would have required the construction of many more of the class. Although they had a 5.5in (140mm) deck gun and two 25mm anti-aircraft guns, the boats also carried torpedo armament, the two tubes fitted in early units soon being removed in an effort to improve the design's poor handling characteristics. The boats were particularly vulnerable once detected, therefore, and nine were lost.

The 'Type KD-6a' class was similar in size and basic capabilities to the 'I-361' class. Two of the class, which was designed for the oceanic attack role, were adapted in the later part of 1942 as supply submarines with the deck gun replaced by a landing craft.

The 'Type D2' or 'I-313' class exchanged endurance for further stowage, but the class extended to a mere two boats. Five of the 'Type D1' class boats were eventually converted to *Kaiten* carriers.

More ambitious were the three boats of the 'I-351' class, also known as the 'Type SH' ('Sen Ho' or 'submarine replenisher') class. Some 364ft 2in (111.00m) long and possessing surfaced/submerged displacements of 3,512/4,290 tons, these boats were the Japanese counterpart of the German 'Type XIV' or 'Milchkühe' ('milch cow') class submarines. They had triple hulls, between two of which could be stowed about 600 tons of aviation spirit for the refuelling of long-range flying boats. Inboard stowage included a comprehensive range of stores, ordnance and even spare crews. Only one of these boats was completed.

'I-400' class
(Japan)

Type: Ocean-going attack submarine

Displacement: 5,223 tons surfaced and 6,560 tons submerged

Dimensions: Length 400ft 0in (121.90m); beam 39ft 4in (12.00m); draught 23ft 0in (7.00m)

Armament: One 5.5in (140mm) gun, ten 25mm AA guns in three twin and four single mountings, three Aichi M6A1 floatplanes with torpedoes and bombs, and eight 21in (533mm) torpedo tubes (all forward) for 20 torpedoes

Propulsion: Four diesel engines delivering 7,750hp (5,780kW) and two electric motors delivering 2,400hp (1,190kW) to two shafts

Performance: Maximum speed 19kt surfaced and 7kt submerged; radius 3,775nm (4,350 miles; 7,000km) surfaced at 14kt and 59.5nm (68 miles; 110km) submerged at 3kt

Complement: 140 including flight detachment

Once it had realised that it could not strike effectively at strategic targets on the western seaboard of the United States by conventional means, the Imperial Japanese navy conceived the notion of using for this task a force of specially designed submarines each carrying a pair of floatplane

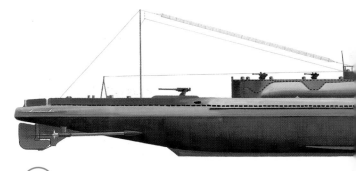

bombers. Because of the ranges involved and the sizeable accommodation required for these warplanes, the boats would have to be large, with considerable beam and length to minimise ship motion during aircraft operations. A capacious hull could be used to add accommodation, and the warplanes could also be employed as scouts. The resulting 'I-400' class design, which was known officially as the 'Type STo' ('Sen-Toku' or 'special submarine') class, was thus expected to combine several functions in the command, attack and reconnaissance roles. The length was 400ft 3in (122.00m), and a satisfactory length/beam ratio would have involved an unacceptably deep hull if constructed as a single cylinder. The pressure hull was therefore constructed as a horizontal figure-eight in section, reinforced for a useful operational diving depth of 330ft (100m).

Like that of most Japanese boats, the submerged performance was not good, and for operations off the American seaboard the boats were equipped with a fixed rather than retractable snorkel system.

The hangar was a separate pressure cylinder accessible from within the hull, and was tilted upward slightly at its forward end to accord with the slope of the catapult track running the length of the foredeck. As completed, the boats had an aircraft complement of three floatplane bombers. The hangar was sited on the centreline, and the long bridge structure on top of it had to be offset to port.

The beam of the boats allowed for two diesel engines on each shaft driving through a common gearbox, but the 'I-400' class units must have been difficult to dive and handle once submerged. In the event, like that of the generally similar 'I-13' class boats, their priority lapsed and only three of the planned 19 boats were completed. The submarines found no effective employment, although one was converted as a fuel carrier, and all were scuttled by the Americans after the war.

The three completed boats of the 'I-400' class were among the largest conventional submarines built, but were too clumsy to be effective in any real combat role. Somewhat surprisingly, all three of these aircraft-launching submarines survived World War II.

'O', 'P' and 'R' classes
(UK)

Type: Sea-going patrol submarine

Displacement: 1,181 tons surfaced and 2,038 tons submerged

Dimensions: Length 283ft 6in (86.41m); beam 29ft 11in (9.12m); draught 13ft 8in (4.17m)

Armament: One 4in (102mm) gun, and eight 21in (533mm) torpedo tubes (six bow and two stern)

Propulsion: Two diesel engines delivering 4,400hp (3,281kW) and two electric motors delivering 1,320hp (984kW) to two shafts

Performance: Maximum speed 11.5kt surfaced and 9kt submerged; radius 11,400nm (13,125 miles; 21,125km) surfaced at 8kt and 52nm (60 miles; 97km) submerged at 4kt

Complement: 53

The 'O' class, later the 'Oberon' class, was developed to replace the ocean-going 'L' class dating from World War I. The boats of this class were classified as overseas patrol submarines; it is interesting to note that, even at the concept stage in 1922, there was a requirement for long range with a view to possible future operations against Japan, which had been one of the Allied powers in World War I. The *Oberon* was laid down by Chatham Dockyard in 1924 as the lead boat and was closely followed by the *Otway* and the *Oxley*, all with an armament of six bow and two stern tubes with a reload for each. The hull was so large that the boats were decidedly lacking in agility and had their speed reduced by a mass of external fittings. Even after the introduction of drag-reducing features such as fairings, the boats scarcely managed their designed surface speed, and failed to reach the required submerged speed.

The hull was fitted with saddle tanks containing most of the ballast capacity: some of these tanks could double as extra fuel tanks, but this practice was unpopular as there was an inevitable leakage of oil through riveted joins. As with the 'L' class boats, a 4in (102mm) gun was fitted in the conning tower to allow the gun to be worked in heavy seas.

Together with the five related 'P' class submarines, the four boats of the 'R' class were redeployed from China to the Mediterranean in 1940, and the only two boats that survived to 1943 were then used for training rather than operational work.

The Perseus was built by Vickers Armstrong's Barrow yard and was launched in May 1929, and the boat was lost in the Mediterranean during December 1941.

The limitations of the 'Oberon' class boats led to the introduction of the improved 'Odin' class to which the above specification applies. The main changes were an increase in length to permit the installation of more powerful machinery and an increase in beam to improve surfaced stability. Completed in 1928–29, these boats were the *Odin*, *Olympus*, *Orpheus*, *Osiris*, *Oswald* and *Otus*. The boats were still subject to oil leakage from their external tanks,

but were generally improved by a considerable tidying of external details. An interesting idea, that was not pursued, was the incorporation of extra accommodation spaces in the upper casing to ease the confines of the crew on extended patrols.

The succeeding 'Parthian' and 'Rainbow' classes were in essence repeats of the 'Odin' class, and construction totalled six examples of each, which differed from each other only in minor details. Two units of the 'Rainbow' class were later cancelled, and the units completed in 1929–30 were the *Parthian, Perseus, Phoenix, Poseidon, Proteus, Pandora, Rainbow, Regent, Regulus* and *Rover*.

Most of the 'O' class boats were in the Far East in September 1939, when World War II started in Europe, but one of those in home waters, the *Oxley*, had the unfortunate distinction of becoming the first British submarine to be lost, when it was torpedoed in error by another British submarine, the *Triton*. Of the 18 boats in these closely related classes, no fewer than 12 were sunk, most of them before the end of 1942 and many in the close confines of the Mediterranean, an operational area for which the boats were completely unsuited.

Seen in Valletta, the capital of Malta, this is one of the nine boats that comprised the two groups of the 'O' class, which served mainly in the Mediterranean during World War II and lost five of its number.

'Porpoise' class
(UK)

Type: Ocean-going minelaying submarine

Displacement: 1,768 tons surfaced and 2,053 tons submerged

Dimensions: Length 289ft 0in (88.09m); beam 29ft 10in (9.09m); draught 16ft 0in (4.88m)

Armament: One 4in (102mm) gun, six 21in (533mm) torpedo tubes (all bow) with 12 torpedoes, and 50 mines

Propulsion: Two diesel engines delivering 3,300hp (2,461kW) and two electric motors delivering 1,630hp (1,215kW) to two shafts

Performance: Maximum speed 15.5kt surfaced and 9kt submerged; radius 11,500nm (13,240 miles; 21,310km) surfaced at 8kt and 66nm (76 miles; 122km) submerged at 4kt

Complement: 59

Based on the 'Parthian' class, whose six units had recently been completed, the submarines of the 'Porpoise' class were specialised minelayers. Whereas the Germans preferred near-vertical mine chutes located inside the pressure hull, the British preferred external stowage despite the attendant risk of damage from overpressure or depth charging. Earlier minelaying classes, such as the 'E' and 'L' classes, had incorporated mine stowage in the saddle tanks on each side but, in the experimental conversion of the M3 during 1921, tracks were laid over the top of the hull along the greater part of the boat's length and inside the free-flooding space contained within an extra-deep casing: an endless-chain mechanism fed the mines through doors right aft as the submarine moved slowly ahead. It was a development of the latter system that was used in the 'Porpoise' class: in the name ship the system extended over about three-quarters of the boat's length, but in the other boats it was longer. The minelaying system added some 54

The Rorqual was the fourth of the six 'Porpoise' class minelaying submarines, and was launched in July 1936 from Vickers Armstrong's Barrow yard.

tons of topweight, making the boats very tender as they surfaced with a full load in a heavy sea. Extra holes in the casing then improved drainage and reduced the flooding time, allowing the boats to dive more quickly.

Launched between 1932 and 1938, the boats were the *Porpoise*, *Grampus*, *Narwhal*, *Rorqual*, *Cachalot* and *Seal*. Three other boats were cancelled.

As weight rather than performance was the critical factor driving the design, the boats were fitted with a small diesel engine of indifferent power, and this resulted in only modest surface speed. To avoid the type of detection from fuel leaks that plagued the submarines of earlier classes, all bunkers were internal although this feature required the downward extension of the pressure hull like a box keelson to meet the saddle tanks. This cross-section limited the boats' diving depth to just 300ft (91m) by comparison with the 500ft (152m) of the boats of the 'Parthian' class.

The primary operational task of the 'Porpoise' class was overtaken by the development of a mine capable of being laid through a conventional torpedo tube, but despite this fact, the class was used for the operational laying of some 2,600 mines. The boats proved invaluable during the height of the siege of Malta in 1942 when, with the available 'O' class submarines, they ferried personnel and supplies to the island's garrison. The *Seal*, unable to dive after being damaged by mines in the Kattegat, was compelled to surrender to a pair of German floatplanes, but was repaired by the Germans for training use as the *UB-A*. Only the *Rorqual* survived World War II.

'S' class
(UK)

Type: Sea-going patrol submarine

Displacement: 860 tons surfaced and 990 tons submerged

Dimensions: Length 217ft 0in (66.14m); beam 23ft 6in (7.16m); draught 10ft 6in (3.20m)

Armament: One 4in (102mm) gun and six 21in (533mm) torpedo tubes, or one 3in (76mm) gun and seven 21in (533mm) torpedo tubes

Propulsion: Two diesel engines delivering 1,900hp (1,417kW) and two electric motors delivering 1,300hp (969kW) to two shafts

Performance: Maximum speed 15kt surfaced and 9kt submerged; radius 7,500nm (8,635 miles; 13,890km) surfaced at 10kt

Complement: 44

Although its design origins can be traced back to 1928, the 'S' class submarine was very successful during World War II and, with 62 such boats completed, was the Royal Navy's most numerous single submarine class. Intended as replacements for the 'H' class boats, the 'S' class submarines possessed the type of performance that permitted operations in the shallow, difficult waters of areas such as the Baltic and the Mediterranean. A surface displacement limit of 600 tons was demanded in an effort to ensure that the resulting submarine was small, but the requirement for the class also demanded the ability to sail 500nm (575 miles; 925km) to and from its operational area, where it was expected to remain for up to 10 days: any increase in the transit range would have presented difficulty, as additional space would have been needed for the bulky radio equipment required to transmit over the greater range.

The specification was later altered dramatically, and demanded 1,050nm (1,210 miles; 1,945km) transit passages at not less than 9kt, followed by eight days on station.

A class of four 'Swordfish' subclass submarines was initially built: launched between 1931 and 1933 by Chatham Dockyard, these boats had a displacement of 640 tons

This is one of the 'S' class submarines that were among the most successful boats operated by the Royal Navy in World War II, when boats of the class's two groups were operated in home waters, the Mediterranean and the Far East.

The two groups of the 'S' class were differentiated by the greater length and displacement of the boats of the second group.

despite a major weight-control effort, and a length of 202ft 6in (61.72m). It was then realised that the design limit was too tight, and it was accordingly relaxed to 670 tons for the eight 'Shark' subclass submarines (built between 1934 and 1937), which had a length of 208ft 9in (63.63m).

It had been planned to terminate production after these 12 boats of what became known as Group 1 of the 'S' class, but the outbreak of World War II and the exigencies of the period led to construction of an improved Group 2 variant with greater length and superior overall capabilities, and it is to this subvariant that the above specification applies.

To save topweight, a 3in (76mm) rather than 4in (102mm) deck gun was fitted but, with the hull lengthened to 217ft 0in (66.14m), it became possible to incorporate an additional torpedo tube aft in some boats. Other boats exchanged both of these features for a single 4in (102mm) deck gun: with a maximum load of only 12 or 13 torpedoes, the gun was very useful for the dispatch of targets such as smaller merchant ships. Earlier boats had fuel tanks within the pressure hull, but later units supplemented these with external capacity, which allowed them to work even in the Far East.

Eight of the original 12 boats were lost, but of the following 50 submarines only eight were sunk. All of the losses in the first group took place before February 1941, while the first hull of succeeding groups was not launched until October 1941.

'T' class
(UK)

Type: Ocean-going patrol submarine

Displacement: 1,325 tons surfaced and 1,570 tons submerged

Dimensions: Length 275ft 0in (83.82m); beam 26ft 7in (8.10m); draught 14ft 9in (4.50m)

Armament: One 4in (102mm) gun, and ten or eleven 21in (533mm) torpedo tubes (10 bow in first group and 8 bow and 3 stern in second group)

Propulsion: Two diesel engines delivering 2,500hp (1,865kW) and two electric motors delivering 1,450hp (1,081kW) to two shafts

Performance: Maximum speed 15.25kt surfaced and 9kt submerged; radius 11,000nm (12,665 miles; 20,380km) surfaced at 10kt

Complement: 56 in the first group and 61 in the second group

Readily identifiable by their unusually cranked profiles, the 'T' class submarines were the Royal Navy's standard war-time patrol submarines: between the initial *Triton* and final *Tabard*, launched in October 1931 and November 1945 respectively, the class reached a respectable 54 in total.

    With the high-speed 'Thames' class abandoned after the completion of only three boats (as a result of excessive topweight sensitivity and because a replacement was required for the unsatisfactory 'O' class), the design of the 'T' class had to rectify the shortcomings of previous classes whilst according with treaty agreements. The London Naval Treaty limited total rather than individual displacement, and an adequate number of new boats could be ensured within the British treaty total only by restriction of individual displacement to 1,000 tons, into which a 42-day endurance had to be packaged. The final result was some 9 per cent heavier than planned, but the design produced submarines of notable reliability and was therefore a major credit to its designers.

Because of their displacement limit, the 'T' class boats could be fitted only with small diesel engines and their surface speed was therefore modest. The boats had a powerful offensive capability, however, as the six 21in (533mm) forward tubes within the pressure hull were complemented by another pair of tubes in the bulged bow casing and a further pair in the casing, one on each side of the conning tower. A 10-torpedo forward salvo could therefore be fired.

This torpedo tube arrangement was standard for the 22 boats built before World War II, but in the later units the amidships tubes were moved farther aft and reversed, while a single tube was added in the casing right aft. War-built boats also had their bows altered to set the external tubes higher, and some of their external ballast tanks were converted into bunker space. This allowed a virtual doubling of oil fuel capacity, and the endurance of the boat was thus greater than that of the crew and their supplies.

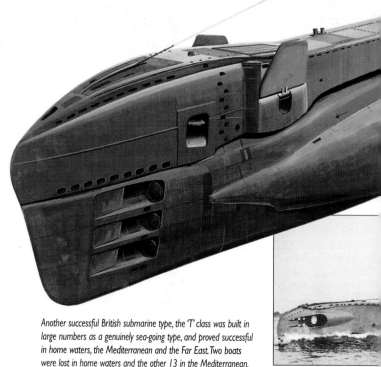

Another successful British submarine type, the 'T' class was built in large numbers as a genuinely sea-going type, and proved successful in home waters, the Mediterranean and the Far East. Two boats were lost in home waters and the other 13 in the Mediterranean.

Fourteen of the boats completed before World War II were sunk, most of them in the Mediterranean. Those from the wartime programmes were completed mainly after the end of the Mediterranean war, and only one of these was lost at sea. After the end of World War II many of the boats were sold, while others were stretched and streamlined to serve beside their 'A' class successors into the late 1960s. A further four boats were cancelled, and another was projected but was never laid down.

Built by Vickers Armstrong, the Truculent *was the penultimate boat of the first group of the 'T' class, and survived World War II only to be lost in an accident during 1950.*

'U' and 'V' classes
(UK)

Type: Coastal patrol submarine

Displacement: 670 tons surfaced and 740 tons submerged

Dimensions: Length 206ft 0in (62.19m); beam 16ft 0in (4.88m); draught 15ft 6in (4.12m)

Armament: One 3in (76mm) gun, and four 21in (533mm) torpedo tubes (all bow) with 8 torpedoes

Propulsion: Two diesel engines delivering 800hp (597kW) and two electric motors delivering 760hp (567kW) to two shafts

Performance: Maximum speed 12.5kt surfaced and 9kt submerged; radius 4,700nm (5,410 miles; 8,710km) surfaced at 10kt and 61nm (70 miles; 113km) submerged at 7kt

Complement: 31

The small submarines of the 'U' class were among the most successful boats operated by the Royal Navy in the Mediterranean, where their small size was an advantage.

The single-hulled 'U' class boats were designed originally as unarmed targets to replace the elderly 'H' class boats, and were a little larger than their predecessors. Three boats were laid down as such but, given the Royal Navy's lack of a modern coastal submarine, it seemed advantageous to modify the bow to take torpedo tubes. As the after end of the hull had a sharp taper and because the casing ended short of the stern, the armament was all located forward as four 21in (533mm) tubes in the pressure hull, and (as an indication of the poor accuracy of the torpedo salvoes of the day) the bow casing was also bulged to take two more tubes. This was not a good design feature, for the modest height of the design resulted in a shallow periscope depth, and the oversize bow casing made it difficult to maintain constant depth and caused a characteristic 'pressure hump' in the water above it: the result of these features was that the 'U' class boats were comparatively easy to see.

At the beginning of World War II a sub-group of 12 more boats was ordered, with a length increase of 5ft 3in (1.60m) to improve the design's lines and to provide more internal volume. Eight of these boats had only four tubes. Some 34 more submarines of this type followed as Group 2 of the 'U' class, and these were characterised by further enhancement of their lines and enlarged bunker space.

Although extremely agile, the 'U' class boats were rather limited in diving depth and had a low surface speed. As a result, the design was further updated to create the 'V' class (whose details are given in the above specification), with an additional mid-body section to accommodate a more powerful propulsion arrangement, and with the hull redesigned to allow both a diving depth of 300ft (91m) rather than the 200ft (61m) of the 'U' class submarines, and to facilitate the use of all-welded construction in modules. Orders were placed for 33 units of the 'V' class, but only 21 of these boats were completed. With the exception of two early units constructed by Chatham Dockyard, all 81 boats were built in the two Vickers Armstrong yards at Barrow and on Tyneside.

The 'U' and 'V' class submarines proved themselves well suited to operations in the shallow and confined waters of the North Sea and the Mediterranean; a total of 19 were lost. After the end of the Mediterranean war the surviving boats had little use, and many were either transferred or reverted to the training role for which the 'U' class had originally been planned.

'Narwhal' class
(USA)

Type: Ocean-going fleet submarine

Displacement: 2,130 tons surfaced and 3,900 tons submerged

Dimensions: Length 370ft 7in (112.95m); beam 33ft 3in (10.13m); draught 15ft 9in (4.80m)

Armament: Two 6in (152mm) guns in single mountings, and six 21in (533mm) torpedo tubes (four bow and two stern) later increased to ten tubes with 40 torpedoes

Propulsion: Four Fairbanks Morse diesel engines delivering 5,400hp (4,027kW) and two Westinghouse electric motors delivering 2,540hp (1,894kW) to two shafts

Performance: Maximum speed 17kt surfaced and 8kt submerged; radius 17,475nm (20,125 miles; 33,355km)

surfaced at 10kt and 50nm (58 miles; 93km) submerged
at 5kt

Complement: 89

The two units of the 'Narwhal' class, which were the
Narwhal and the *Nautilus* built respectively by Portsmouth
and Mare Island Navy Yards for completion in the early
1930s, should be classed as a group with the *Argonaut* that
immediately preceded them. The origins of these three
boats can be traced to the considerable impression made
on the US Navy by the large transport submarines with
which the German navy worked the United States' eastern
seaboard during World War I. The US Navy was now
switching its attention from coastal submarine operations
off the western seaboard of the United States to oceanic
submarine operations in the Pacific Ocean. In the early
1920s, therefore, a number of semi-experimental
submarines for the minelaying role appeared: the *V-4* (later
Argonaut) and two cruiser submarines, the *V-5* (later
Narwhal) and the *V-6* (later *Nautilus*). These boats were all

*The Narwhal was a very large ocean-going
submarine that, with its sister ship
Nautilus, was found to be too large for
effective use in World War II.
Complementing six 21in (533mm) torpedo
tubes, the deck armament comprised two
6in (152mm) guns.*

very large by the standards of the day; even the later boats, which were 10ft 6in (3.20m) shorter than the *Argonaut*, were longer than the French *Surcouf*. As a minelayer, the *V-4* could ship 60 mines laid through two tubes exiting beneath the counter.

Forward of the engine room's after bulkhead the two 'Narwhal' class submarines were virtually identical, mounting two torpedo tubes aft in place of the mine stowage. The torpedo stowage was large, in order to provide a good match for the boats' considerable radius and endurance, and amounted to more than 36 such weapons carried both inside the hull and on the casing. To stretch the boats' offensive capability still further by reducing demand for torpedoes, two 6in (152mm) deck guns were mounted, and these were the largest-calibre deck guns ever installed in an American submarine. The task of scouting for targets was initially allocated to a small floatplane, the plans for which were later dropped.

All three boats were considered slow by US standards but, although all scheduled for revision with a higher-rated propulsion arrangement, only the *Nautilus* was modified by the outbreak of World War II. The *Nautilus* was fitted with two extra tubes in the after casing, and the other two boats gained four more tubes in the amidships casing, two firing forward and two firing aft.

Despite the US Navy's acute shortage of submarines in 1942, these three boats were considered too slow and vulnerable for combat patrols and were modified in various degrees for clandestine operations, mostly involving the running of personnel and supplies, and for which they were well suited by reason of their considerable internal volume. The *Nautilus* had facilities for refuelling long-range seaplanes, but was not used in this role during the war. All three boats operated particularly between their west Australian bases and the Philippines. The *Nautilus* finished the stricken Japanese carrier *Soryu* after the Battle of Midway in June 1942, and then landed personnel on an unoccupied island near Tarawa to build a secret airstrip. Other raids were carried out on Makin Island and Attu Island in the Aleutians. The *Argonaut* was lost in 1943.

New 'S' class
(USA)

Type: Ocean-going fleet submarine

Displacement: 1,440 tons surfaced and 2,200 tons submerged

Dimensions: Length 308ft 0in (93.88m); beam 26ft 2in (7.98m); draught 14ft 3in (4.34m)

Armament: One 3in (76mm) gun later upgraded to one 4in (102mm) gun in most boats, and eight 21in (533mm) torpedo tubes (four bow and four stern) with 24 torpedoes

Propulsion: Four HOR or General Motors diesel engines delivering 5,500hp (4,101kW) and four Elliot Motor electric motors delivering 2,660hp (1,984kW) to two shafts

Performance: Maximum speed 21kt surfaced and 9kt submerged; radius 10,000nm (11,515 miles; 18,530km) surfaced at 10kt and 85nm (98 miles; 158km) submerged at 5kt

Complement: 15

Known as the New 'S' class because the early units took the pendants of the Old 'S' class boats still in service, these 16 boats were built by Electric Boat, Portsmouth Navy Yard and Mare Island Navy Yard in two very similar groups of six and 10 boats respectively. The design of the New 'S' class was modelled closely upon that of the preceding 1,320-ton 'P' class, but differed most notably in possessing a deeper stern that permitted an increase in the number of after torpedo tubes from two to four.

The 10 boats of the 'P' class and the units of the succeeding New 'S' class were the first submarines of all-welded construction to be built for the US Navy and, despite the fact that the technique was still under development, the workmanship was notably sound as revealed by the survival of the *Salmon* (SS182), lead boat of the Group I subclass of the New 'S' class and to which the above specification applies: the boat was severely depth-charged in October 1944 by four Japanese escorts after having torpedoed a tanker off Kyushu: the combination of concussion and overpressure effects through being driven far below design depth left the hull dished between frames, but the submarine nonetheless managed to return to base even though it was then deemed irreparable and was scrapped. This level of survivability was a function of the double hull generally used in American submarines, for it constituted a protective feature if the ballast and fuel tanks between the outer and inner hulls had an ullage space over the liquid contents.

Some of the boats were fitted with a composite propulsion system: in this type of system, the two forward diesel engines drove generators directly and the two after units were geared to the shafts, the gearing being shared by the electric propulsion motors on each shaft. The arrangement was complicated but proved satisfactory in service.

Twelve reload torpedoes were located within the pressure hull, with another four weapons in external stowage in the casing, but this was an arrangement that proved itself vulnerable to the effects of depth-charge attack. As an alternative to the internally carried or stowed torpedoes, each boat could carry mines (two mines instead of one torpedo) that were laid through the tubes. The boats were fitted initially with one 3in (76mm) deck gun, but this was replaced by a 4in (102mm) weapon in most boats. Wartime adaptation was evidenced by the cutting down of the large 'sail' type of conning tower to a profile similar to that of later classes.

The boats of Group 2 of the New 'S' class included the *Squalus* (SS192), which foundered as a result of an induction valve failure whilst on trials in May 1939. The boat was salvaged and refitted, and survived World War II as the *Sailfish*. The *Swordfish* (SS193) was credited with the first Japanese merchantman sunk by the American forces in World War II.

'Gato' and 'Balao' classes
(USA)

Type: Ocean-going fleet submarine

Displacement: 1,525 tons surfaced and 2,415 tons submerged

Dimensions: Length 311ft 9in (95.02m); beam 27ft 3in (8.31m); draught 15ft 3in (4.65m)

Armament: One 5in (127mm) gun, and ten 21in (533mm) torpedo tubes (six bow and four stern) with 24 torpedoes

Propulsion: Four Fairbanks Morse, General Motors or HOR diesel engines delivering 5,400hp (4,027kW) and four General Electric, Elliot Motor or Allis-Chalmers electric motors delivering 2,740hp (2,043kW) to two shafts

Performance: Maximum speed 20kt surfaced and 8.5kt submerged; radius 11,500nm (13,245 miles; 21,315km) surfaced at 10k and 95nm (109 miles; 175km) submerged at 5kt

Complement: 80

Built by the Mare Island Navy Yard and launched in August 1944, the 'Balao' class submarine Springer (SS414) survived World War II.

The Americans developed the 'T' class design from the New 'S' class design, and 12 of these boats were launched in 1940 by Electric Boat, Portsmouth Navy Yard and Mare Island Navy Yard. The boats differed from their immediate predecessors mainly in having two extra 21in (533mm)

The 'Gato' class boat was one of the Americans' war-winning weapons of World War II, its capabilities and availability in large numbers allowing the US Navy's submarine force to decimate the Japanese merchant marine as well as attacking warships.

torpedo tubes forward for a total of 10 tubes, and later in having a specially modified 5in (127mm) deck gun in place of the earlier 4in (102mm) or 3in (76mm) weapons. This process of gradual evolutionary design was highly successful, and resulted in a submarine with operational characteristics fully acceptable for the Pacific campaign of World War II. What was needed in this campaign was a remarkable combination of reliability and radius/endurance, the latter measured in terms of consumables such as fuel, torpedoes and food: because of the distances involved in patrols across the Pacific Ocean, the required endurance was much greater than that typical of operations in the European theatre, and also meant that more boats were required to keep an adequate number of submarines on station.

The 'Gato' class was an improved version of the 'T' class, and went into large-volume production in a number of yards. The first unit of the class was the *Drum* (SS228), which

By comparison with the slightly later 'Balao' class development of the same basic design, the 'Gato' class submarine had a hull of weaker steel that resulted in a diving depth of 300ft (91m) rather than 400ft (122m), although for reasons of morale this fact was not revealed to the crews of the boats.

was completed shortly before the start of hostilities, when operations soon revealed that the boats, while officially rated for a maximum diving depth of 300ft (91m), were in fact capable of operating at greater depths when the situation demanded.

The earlier boats had a large 'sail' type of conning tower similar in appearance to those of pre-war designs. The size of the sail was soon reduced as boats came in for repair, but although the structure could be lowered, the very high support structure required by the long periscopes remained a lofty feature. Operating on the surface more than would have been possible in European waters, the boats also began to accumulate varied outfits of regular and non-regular automatic weapons for defence against Japanese warplanes, and these weapons demanded the addition of various platforms to support them. Some boats even gained an additional main-calibre deck gun so that there was less demand on the 24 torpedoes that were generally shipped.

After the completion of an initial 73 boats, the hull was secretly improved by the adoption of high-tensile steels and advanced sections, increasing the official diving limit of the relevant boats to 400ft (122m). No less than 256 of these improved boats were ordered as the 'Balao' class, but only 122 were actually completed.

The combined 'Gato' and 'Balao' classes formed the highly effective backbone of the US Navy's submarine strength in World War II. The boats were instrumental in the defeat of Japan, for their operations in the central and western areas of the Pacific interdicted and, finally, all but severed Japan's lines of communications between the home islands and the various parts of the 'Greater East Asia Co-prosperity Sphere', effectively halting the outward flow of men and equipment from Japan, and the inward flow of fuel oil and raw materials. In the process of this highly effective campaign, 29 of the boats were lost. After World War II the US Navy learned much from examination of captured German submarines about the ways in which underwater performance could be enhanced, and many of the boats were accordingly modernised under the GUPPY (Greater Underwater Propulsive Efficiency) programmes. These updated boats remained the core of the US Navy's submarine capability until the introduction of nuclear-powered submarines from the mid-1950s, and sub-stantial numbers of GUPPY-modernised submarines are still in service with the navies of smaller nations.

'Tench' class
(USA)

Type: Ocean-going fleet submarine

Displacement: 1,510 tons surfaced and 2,415 tons submerged

Dimensions: Length 311ft 7in (95.0m); beam 27ft 3in (8.31m); draught 15ft 3in (4.65m)

Armament: One or two 5in (127mm) guns in single mountings, and ten 21in (533mm) torpedo tubes (six bow and four stern) with 28 torpedoes

Propulsion: Four Fairbanks Morse or General Motors diesel engines delivering 5,400hp (4,027kW) and two General Electric, Elliot Motor or Westinghouse electric motors delivering 2,740hp (2,043kW) to two shafts

Performance: Maximum speed 20kt surfaced and 9kt submerged; radius 11,500nm (13,240 miles; 21,315km) surfaced at 10kt and 110nm (127 miles; 204km) submerged at 4kt

Complement: 81

By the last month of World War II, when this photograph of a 'Tench' class submarine was taken, American submarines were able to operate mostly on the surface because Japanese aircraft were scarce.

The 'Tench' class should be considered as the final refinement of the basic American fleet submarine design whose ancestry could be traced back to the 'P' class boats. Externally, the 'Tench' class submarines were virtually identical to the 'Balao' class submarines, and so closely related were the two types that some of the later 'Balao' contracts were converted to the 'Tench' class. Although 25 boats had been completed by the end of World War II, most of these were still working up in home waters and only a few of the boats therefore saw operational service, in which none of the class was lost. Production totalled 33 boats completed between 1944 and 1946, with another 101 cancelled or scrapped incomplete.

Although they were not obvious, the differences between the 'Tench' class and its predecessors were significant. The first of these differences concerned the propulsion arrangement. In the 'Balao' class the four diesels each ran a directly coupled generator, which served for both battery charging and powering of the electric propulsion motors when surfaced. Each shaft had two motors, coupled to it via reduction gearing: the high-speed motors and the reduction gear were both noisy; the reduction gears were

also expensive, temperamental, liable to damage and, in traditional production terms, an item that often occasioned delays in the completion of units. It was therefore sensible to develop a large and slow-turning motor that could be coupled directly.

The fuel and ballast tanks of the 'Tench' class boats were better organised than those of earlier classes, mainly to obviate the requirement to duct the ballast-tank vents through the pressure hull (where they constituted a flooding hazard), and also to provide better compensation for the considerable change in weight and trim as stores were consumed during an extended patrol. The designers also created the volume for another four reload torpedoes which, in combination with radar and a capable mechanical fire-control computer, made the 'Tench' class boats even more advanced than their Japanese counterparts. Finally, in an effort to improve on the relatively slow diving time of 55–60 seconds, the casings of the boats were penetrated with even more holes than had been employed in earlier classes.

The Argonaut of the 'Tench' class was typical of its type, with a 5in (127mm) deck gun abaft the conning tower and provision for a similar weapon forward of the tower, which carried one 40mm Bofors gun and two 20mm Oerlikon cannon for the anti-aircraft role.